Speed Queens

Danica Patrick is from the United States. Milka Duno is from Venezuela. Laleh Seddigh is from Iran. They race cars and they are the best women racers in their countries. But their road to success was difficult.

Why was this? "Racing is for men," some male drivers said, and they were not always friendly. But this did not stop the speed queens. Their success is important for women in sport—and to many people's lives.

Danica Patrick: The Little Racer

Danica Patrick is not very tall but her name is big in racing.

"Go, Danica!" people call at an Indy 300* race in Japan in 2008.

She finishes in first place. She is the first female winner of an Indy car race. Some male drivers are unhappy about this: "She's quick because she's small and light. We're heavy and that's difficult for us."

But Danica does not listen. "These people don't want to finish after a woman," she says. "And there are small men, too!"

Danica started to race in 1992. She was only ten years old. She raced very small open cars for young people. Her family did not have a lot of money but they loved racing.

"I can build the cars for you," her father, T.J., said.

---

* Indy 300 and 500: important American races for big cars, with circuits in the United States, Canada, Australia, and ⌐

"My father was very important to me," Danica says. "He was my teacher, my engineer, and my friend."

Two years later, Danica was a champion in small cars. But she wanted to race big sports cars, too.

"Where can I find a good teacher?" she asked T.J., some years later.

"In England," was the answer. She moved there in 1997.

Danica's teacher in England was the famous racing driver Jackie Stewart. Jackie was a good teacher but some of the male students were not very friendly.

"I was often unhappy at that difficult time because I was away from my family," Danica says. "But I'm a strong person."

In October 2000, she finished second in England's Formula Ford Festival race. No American—man or woman—before Danica had this success.

She went home in 2001. Now she was famous.

"A woman driver is one of our best racers," many Americans said.

But did important people in racing think that, too? Yes—Bobby Rahal, an Indy 500 champion, wanted Danica in his 2002 team.

All important championship races in the United States are for men and women. There are usually thirty or forty drivers in one race. In that year, Danica was one of only two women. The second was Sarah Fisher.

"Can one of them win?" people asked.

Danica answered their question in her first race. This was in Long Beach, California. She finished in first place.

It was her first important win and she was only twenty years old.

The years 2002–04 were all good years for Danica.

T.J. and Bobby Rahal were very happy.

"In the new year, you're going to be in the Indy 500 races," Bobby said.

The best male drivers in the United States all race in the Indy races. In 2005, Danica raced with them for the first time. In her first race, she started and finished at number four. Danica did not win an Indy race in 2005 or 2006 but her name was always with the year's ten best drivers.

Danica's team

Happy with success

Racing was not all about success. There were unhappy times, too. Her friend Paul Dana was in a race in Miami. On the circuit before the race, a driver had a problem with his car. Dana was behind him and went into the car. Two hours later, he was dead.

In 2007, Danica left Bobby and went to the famous Andretti racing team. She and Bobby stayed good friends but the problems with some of the male drivers did not stop.

"Sometimes, Danica drives slowly and gives us no room on the road," they said. "She's never going to win an Indy race."

They were wrong. In the Indy Japan 300 in Motegi, Danica finished first. A lot of very good male drivers never have this success.

The 2008 races finished with Danica at number six of the year's best drivers. To many Americans, she was the "Sportswoman of the Year."

From 2005, Danica Patrick was very famous. She was a beautiful woman and she raced with the best men drivers. She was on TV programs and in the newspapers. A lot of people watched racing because of Danica.

"How were you successful?" they asked.

Danica answered their questions in her book *Danica: Crossing the Line*. It was the story of her life. T.J. and her mother were very important to her success, she said. Now racing makes her happy and brings her a lot of money.

"Racing is not about men or women," she says. "We know that now. It is about good drivers."

But success comes and goes. All racing drivers know that. What can they do after racing?

"I want to work with young people," Danica says, "because many people worked with me."

Milka Duno: The Late Racer

Milka Duno is from Caracas, Venezuela. She is an engineer with degrees from universities in Venezuela and Spain. Her education was important to her family and she only started to race at twenty-four years old.

Schoolwork was always important to Milka and she was a very good student. She started school in 1976, at four years old. After a short time, her teacher called her "the best student."

"I loved to read," Milka says. "On vacation, my bag was always heavy with books."

After school, she went to university in Caracas. Then she went to the University of Madrid. By 1996, she had four degrees. She was an engineer, too.

To many Venezuelans, engineering was a man's job. But for Milka, all jobs were open to all people. She was an engineer because she loved cars.

"I liked to look at their engines," Milka says. "And I always wanted to drive and race cars. One of my role models was the Finnish racing champion Mika Hakkinen. I wanted his success."

A racing teacher was important but there were not many good teachers in Caracas.

"*I* was my teacher," Milka says. "But I was not always a good student." She remembers, and smiles. "Sometimes, young Milka went up and down the roads near her house in her mother's car. But she didn't ask her mother first!"

After university, Milka was a very good driver. She had a car from her mother and father, and she was very happy.

One day, she and some friends went to a race circuit and she raced cars for the first time. For Milka, that day was very important. It was the start of a new life.

"I loved the noise of the engines," Milka says. "And I loved to drive quickly."

She started to race and she did very well. In 1996, she raced in the important Venezuelan GT Championship. This was for sports cars. There were a lot of very good male drivers in the race but Milka finished second.

"Racing is the job for me," she said.

Her mother and father were not very happy about this. But Milka was now an engineer.

"With no success in racing, there is always a job in engineering for me," she said.

"Racing is the job for me."

After this, her mother and father did not stop their daughter racing. But Milka did not want to stay in Venezuela.

"There are no good racing schools here," she said. "The United States is the place for me."

In 1999, she said goodbye to her family and went to the Skip Barber Racing School in the United States. Her teacher for that year was Chris Mitchum. In 2000, she was in her first race in the United States. She was twenty-eight years old. Success did not come in that race but it came later in the year. She raced in the Ferrari Challenge for small sports cars and she won. She was the first female winner of that race.

For three years she was in a lot of important races and she did very well. But there were no wins in those years. Her first big win came in 2004. She was the first female winner of the Homestead-Miami Speedway race.

Two years later, her best race was the 24 Hours of Daytona. This is a very difficult race for thirty or forty sports cars. Teams of drivers do not stop racing for twenty-four hours, and many cannot finish. Milka and her team came in at number eight.

A lot of big race car teams wanted Milka. In 2007, she was one of the SAMAX Motorsport team's best drivers. In that year's 24 Hours of Daytona race she finished second. This was the best finish for a female driver in that race.

"Milka is a very good driver," people said. "But can she move up to the Indy races and win?"

Her first Indy races were not successful. She had engine problems and some of the male drivers were unhappy with her.

"She's slow," they said. "One of us is going to hit her car one day."

The 24 Hours of Daytona circuit

"Are the Indy races right for Milka?" people asked.

Then, in the Chicagoland Speedway race, she finished at number fifteen of forty drivers.

In 2008, Milka was a driver with the Dreyer and Reinbold Racing Team. She raced very well but again there were engine problems with some of her cars. For the second time, her best race was the Chicagoland Speedway. She finished at number fourteen.

"Sometimes, the best things in life come late," Milka says.

Racing is not the only important thing in Milka's life. In 2008, she was in the movie *Speed Racer*. "Speed" is a young racing driver. He wants to win an important race. In the movie, Milka plays a driver in the same race.

Milka loves her racing and her movie work. She loves children, too.

A role model for children

"Many families do not have much money," she says, "but their children want good jobs. Education is very important for them."

The American program MANA Milka Way, with Wal-Mart stores, gives money for children's education. Milka works with the program and she is the children's role model for success.

"After my racing life finishes, I want a family and children," Milka says. "Then I can be an engineer again, or a racing teacher. I can do this because of my education. You can only have success in sport for a short time. Education is for life."

Laleh Seddigh: On the Streets of Tehran

Laleh Seddigh and Milka Duno have degrees in engineering. Their families had the money for a good education for their daughters. But Laleh's father, Morsal, was happy with her work in racing, too.

"He called me his 'Little Schumacher,'" Laleh says. "He and Michael Schumacher were my role models."

Laleh is from Iran, a very difficult country for drivers. In winter, it is very cold; in summer, it is very hot. There are a lot of cars in the streets of Tehran, and they move slowly. But not Laleh Seddigh.

"I always drive quickly to my work at the university," she says. "Male drivers sometimes get angry with me. But that's not important. I love speed and I want to drive well. That's important to me."

Laleh is now a teacher at Tehran University. She has degrees in sports and engineering.

"I love my university work," she says. "But racing is my first love."

Laleh had two teachers: her father, Morsal, and the streets of Tehran. She started to drive in 1990. She was thirteen years old. At weekends, Morsal went with her. But she sometimes went across Tehran and back in his car after school, too. At the time, Morsal did not know.

Laleh started to race at twenty-three. She raced small cars across country in three-day races. She often won but after some time she wanted to drive big cars on race circuits.

In Iran, there are men's sports and there are sports for women. But the sport of racing is for men *and* women.

A lot of men do not like this. The authorities often stop women racing. They wanted to stop Laleh and this made her father very angry. "I want to move from Iran," he said, but the authorities did not want this. Morsal had a lot of money and he was good for the country.

After three years, the authorities said yes to Laleh. It was early in 2005 and Iran's big championship was in March.

Before the championship, Laleh raced day and night. She wanted to be the best. The day of the race came. She was the only female driver.

Some men smiled. "A woman can't win," they said.

A woman can win!

Iran's champion

They were wrong. Laleh won the race. She was Iran's first female winner. In the same year, she won a race across country for sports cars, too.

Her success did not stop. In 2007, she was second in the championship. But then there was a big problem.

In December, Laleh was in a race for cars with 1600cc* engines and there was a problem with her car. The engineers looked at it and Laleh went into the race again in a second car. Later, the racing authorities looked at the engine of that second car.

---

* 1600cc, 2400cc: These engines are important for the speed of a car. 2400cc is a big engine.

"This is not a 1600cc engine," they said. "It's a 2400cc engine. Now you cannot race for twelve months."

Laleh was angry. "They were wrong," she said to the newspapers. "They want to stop women racing."

Morsal talked to the authorities but their answer was the same.

For a year, Laleh did not race in Iran but she worked at her driving every day. "I want to win again," she said.

Laleh Seddigh's story is now famous. In 2008, there was a BBC television program about her life: *Girl Racer*. Hollywood wants to make a movie about her. The U.S. racing authorities were happy about her racing—and there is a lot of money in American racing. But Laleh wanted to stay in Iran.

"I love my family and my country," she says. "And I have a good job at the university. For now, racing can wait."

"You Can Do It!"

In racing, men and women race in the same championships. They cannot do that in many sports. The three speed queens are very successful. Danica, Milka, and Laleh wanted to be the best and they are queens of the racing circuits. They are winners, and they are role models for women in racing.

But to them success is not only about racing. Education is important, too—and success in life.

We often hear the question: "I want to be one of the best. Can I do it?"

Some people are always going to say, "No, you can't."

The speed queens say, "Don't listen. Yes, you can!"

ACTIVITIES

Pages 1–7

Before you read

1. Look at the photos in the book. Who are these women? Where are they from? What do they do? What do you think?
2. Look at the Word List at the back of the book. What are the words in your language?
3. In your country, are there any sports for men and women in the same game? Why (not)?

While you read

4. Finish these sentences. Write one word.
   a. Danica started to race at .... years old.
   b. Her ...., T.J., was her first teacher.
   c. Her first important win was in Long Beach, in ....
   d. She won her first .... race in Japan.
   e. *Danica: Crossing the Line* is the story of her ....
   f. Milka was an .... because she loved cars.
   g. She started to race .... university.
   h. She was the first .... winner of the Ferrari Challenge.

After you read

5. Work with a friend.
   a. *Student A:* You are T.J. Patrick. Danica is in England. Call her and ask questions about her life there.

      Student B: You are Danica Patrick. Talk to your father.
   b. *Student A:* You are Milka Duno. You want to be a racing driver. Talk to your mother or father about this.

      Student B: You are Milka's mother or father. Milka can have a good job in engineering. Talk to her.

Pages 8–14

Before you read

6 Talk about these questions. What do you think?

  a Milka Duno was in the 24 Hours of Daytona race. What do drivers do in this race?

  b Look at the picture of Laleh Seddigh on page 12. Why did she have problems with racing in her country?

While you read

7 Finish the sentences with one of the numbers.

  2005 2400 2004 24 23 13

  a Milka's first big win was in ....

  b In the Daytona race, teams drive for .... hours.

  c Laleh started to drive at .... years old.

  d She started to race at .... years old.

  e Laleh was the Iranian champion in ....

  f The Iranian authorities stopped Laleh racing because her car had a .... cc engine.

After you read

8 Talk about these questions.

  a Which story do you like best: Danica's, Milka's, or Laleh's? Why?

  b What do you want to do in life? Can you do it? How?

9 What do you think about the sport of racing? Do you watch it? Do you race? Why (not)? Write about it.

10 Who is your role model? Why? Write about that person.